*to Sa...*
*Thanks ...*
*it possible.*
*Love Dad xxx*

# DAISIES IN THE LAWN

*1 October 2023*

## David Thornton

**D & J Thornton**

*This publication would not have been possible without the help and encouragement of my family, for which I am eternally grateful.*

# CONTENTS

# PREFACE

For over sixty years I have observed and written about people, places and events that have made a lasting impression on me.

Born in a working-class area of Leeds I saw the struggles people experienced and the challenging lives they led. For many years as a teacher and then head teacher of an inner city school I saw the extreme difficulties many families faced as well as the moments of happiness some found. There was light at times as well as darkness.

They are nameless people, their voices are silent, their tales are untold. I call them *Daisies in the Lawn* for, like daisies in a well-kept lawn they are ignored and rejected by society, yet they have their own unique beauty and resilience. I wish to let their voices be heard, let their feelings be known.

The selection compiled here includes poems written over decades, sometimes based on people I have known well, sometimes passing acquaintances or people others have told me about. Some are clearly of their time; others are timeless.

I hope you will find beacons of light and strength from these remarkable people as I have.

# BEGINNING

Unknown,
They are the silent ones;
Shadows from the wasteland of want,
Young souls, old souls, scarred souls;
Never belonging,
Lost in the wilderness of their hopeless being,
Locked in the solitude of their worthlessness.
Unwanted –
Like daisies in the well-kept lawn.

# NEVER ONE
# OF THEM

I see the child in the playground
Standing silent, watching the world laugh by.
Bustling boys and girls celebrating fifteen minutes freedom from
the drudgery of books
And he not one of them,
Never one them.

Lives with his aunt
Since his mother went away.
Had no father – none that he ever knew.

Remembered his mother,
Remembered her perfume smelling sweet.
Remembered her buying him Mars bars when they went to Asda
before he started school.

Then one morning she was gone.
His aunt told him never mind, he would see her again one day.

He did see her again one day;
On the pavement by the Post Office.
Followed her home to a strange street he did not know,

Went back four nights, one after the other,
Standing by the betting shop on the corner,
Looking up at the house where she lived.

At last she came out and asked him what he wanted.

He said he didn't know.
She told him to *Piss off*.

# JENNY

Her name was Jenny;
Thirteen years of age,
Mind of an eight year-old.
Hesitating over words mastered the day before,
Reversing her bees and dees in the wayward script she scribbled,
Soiling her exercise book with grubby, sticky fingers.

Hair lank, lice infested;
Cut by her mother jagged and short.
Her dress shining-stained with the dinner droppings of meals long gone.
When she passed by my office, the stench of stale urine hung in the air long after she had disappeared from view.
She wore trainers, I remember,
Stuffing paper in the holes to keep out the winter rains and snow.

We gave her some shoes – a teacher's daughter had grown out of them.
She wore them once to school
And then arrived in her trainers ever after.

In summer she took library books home.
They came back unread, smeared with jam or treacle.
In winter she never bothered;
You can't look at books by candle-light when they turn the electric off.
They kept warm with a paraffin heater her mother had been given.

Most times they ate tinned beans and sausages or spread tomato sauce on a slice of bread;

On good days, when they could afford it, they had a fish-cake and chips and a cream bun.

Her mother said it would be bette when Ben got out.

Until then they sat at night on the bed in the corner and dreamed dreams of winning the lottery.
They never did the lottery,
Just dreamed dreams.

Tomorrow all would be well.
But where was her tomorrow?

# GREEN FIELDS AND RAINBOWS

They crouch under the table, these sisters
Trying not to hear.
The mother shrieking;
The man's voice, vicious and slurred.

Tony frightened them —
He was all right when he gave them money for crisps and Coke
But he was nasty when he shouted,

The tattoo round his neck that said *Cut here*
It went deep, dark red when he shouted like that.
They closed their eyes, these sisters, and clenched their teeth.
It's safer with the eyes closed,
Nothing can get you when the eyes are closed.

And the ranting, and the shouting, and the screaming goes on.
*You drunken swine!*
The bangs and bumps and cries and crash of crockery.
*You filthy, bastard!*
*Whoring, bitch!*
The windows shake as the door slams.

I see them struggle in the early morning light down the street,
The girls each carrying a plastic bag, the mother, bruised within
and without, holds the baby and a small suitcase,

Looking for sanctuary, refuge.
They find it in the big house with the overgrown garden.

The battered wives' home in Bedlington Place

Trish had red and blue hair in plaits and a cigarette in her mouth.
*Be safe here*, she said.
*No men allowed in here*, she said.
*All men  are bastards.*

There were women there, and children;
Drawn-faced women,
Sad-faced women,
Harsh-faced women.
The children snot-nosed and grimy,
Eyes tired, hinting the look of the hunted.

It wasn't home.
Not like their home.
The cooker caked with the debris of long-gone meals,
The sink blocked,
The lavatory unflushed.
But closing their eyes
They saw green fields and rainbows.

# COPPER KELLY

Every Saturday home game we went;
Running down the snicket to make our footfalls echo,
Then crossing the wasteground by the railway cutting where the
rosebay willowherb bloomed and the ragman tethered his horse.

At the main road we met the crowds,
Stoop shouldered and wrapped against the autumn wind and
winter's icy chills.
Forward relentlessly they swept, pace never changing,
Caps pulled down, raincoats belted,
Smoking Robins or Woodbines, one after another.

Through clicking turnstiles they went,
Onto cinder terraces with rotted wooden steps
And there waited for kick-off time to come.

But we, pocketless of a penny,
Walked by the wooden boundary of the ground
Seeking open sesame – the loose plank in the fence.

We paused when Copper Kelly swayed passed us, chewing a piece
of liquorice as he went.
He clasped his hands behind him underneath his cape
And sniffed as he went by.
We took off his swaying walk behind his back and laughed to
ourselves that *Kelly was a-nelly-with-a-big-fat-belly.*

At the end of the fence he stopped.
If he'd turned he would have caught climbing through,
But Kelly was a nelly

Preoccupied with the line of empty trams waiting for the final whistle to blow.
For full five minutes he absorbed himself in empty trams;
Every home match the same.

Finally, he turned and looked our way.
But we were in!
What a nelly-with-a-belly not to know! we laughed.

And we never realised
Until we grew up.

# BABY PETER

It all happened a long time ago, as I remember.
The grownups had spoken in hushed tones
And nodded
And fell silent when we came in.

Mabel opposite grew round bellied.
I remember they said she had been to London with a soldier.
I never saw the soldier.
But Mabel had a tight round belly
And one day she had a
Baby.

They called him Peter.
They let us see him, pink faced and tiny
And he cried with a weak, shrill cry.

It was dark in their house, I remember.
The damp clothes hanging on a line over the fireplace stank
And a wooden clock above the sideboard ticked ceaselessly.

I remember the women in the street, shaking their heads.
They said it was terrible that the district nurse had caught Peter's
arm with a scalding hot kettle.
And he had such a *bronchial* cough.

I remember the dark clouds rolling in from the south-west that
Tuesday afternoon when the doctor's car pulled up.
I remember the rain spinning like pennies on tarmac'd Whingate
Road.
I remember the crash of thunder across the heavens

The moment Peter died.

It was such a long, long time ago;
A long, long time ago.

Half a century of wars and assassinations, of men walking on the
Moon, of empires waxing and waning, of great freedoms heralded
and great dreams destroyed –
And yet, I still remember Peter.

I remember the undertaker carrying Peter's tiny coffin under his
arm like a box of unwanted books.
I wondered then as a boy why he had ever been born –
Only to suffer.

I still wonder.

# EBONY

He  shared a corner of the playground alone with himself,
Silent in the hubbub of the boys' yard,
Watching what went on,
Never part of it.

I remember his face, ebony black it was.
They called him Ebony.
He didn't mind.
Just stood in silence and ignored them
Dressed in the cast-offs of cousins;
Trousers cut down to fit with a pair of scissors that left the
bottoms frayed,
Jacket patched and buttonless.
The last of eight,

He slept during his early years in a drawer taken each night from
the sideboard.

When his mother couldn't cope,
Went to live with his grandmother and four older cousins.

On dark nights when the winter winds whipped the chimney
stack
And rattled the attic windows
He sat on his grandmother's bed and listened to tales of Antigua;
Of roaming the rugged coastline and smelling the smoke of the
charcoal burners,
Of pineapples and sugarcane,
Of chasing the horse drawn carts down the main street of St John
And how the bishop patted her head for knowing the Lord's Prayer

when she was just six.

He never went on a holiday, as I remember, until the school
arranged it.
Twenty-two children off to the country for a week
Paid for by a local charity.
He, bringing his belongings in a cardboard box tied with string,
was laughed at by the rest.
He said nothing,
Looked imperiously around
And sat alone in the coach.

He was not part of their world
More a drifting spirit from another age, another existence,
Seeking its soul
And waiting patiently for better times to come.

# BLOODY SCHOOL

I hate that bloody school.
I hate them bloody teachers that talk posh.
I hate them bloody lessons.
I hate bloody science.
*The-formula-of-ionic-compounds is a title; under-line-it-with-a-double-line!*
I don't know what the hell he means.
And he breathes tobaccoy breath from his yellow moustache and spits when he talks.

They laughed at me in Geography.
I didn't know cereals grew in fields. I thought they were on tele.
Well, they are on our tele.
*Dallas* is a serial.
My mam likes *Dallas*. I don't.
I think they look daft in them big hats.
I didn't know cereals were cornflakes.

I like cornflakes, cornflakes with sugar on.
Sugar you bugger.
Old Watsons a bugger.
*Get-on-yer-hind-legs-boy!*
I hate bloody Watson and his bloody maths.
He hates me cos I can't do his bloody silly sums.
All them numbers.
*Don't-you-know-seven-nines-at-your-age-boy?*
Do I hell!
Our kid  knows seven-nines but he nicks off school.
My mam says she's going to kill him,  but she won't.

She's too busy with Gus.

I don't like Gus.
He's not like them others she used to know.
He's got tattoos all over his arms
And he never gives us nowt to go out of the house like them others
did.
She's allus shouting and screaming at Gus.

I hate it when they start shouting and screaming.
He  thumped her once.
He was drunk and then she clawed  his  face and it bled and he fell
down.
She didn't knock him down.
He was just drunk.
Spewed up all  over  our tele.
I was watching *Startrek*.

When  they  start shouting and bawling our little Maureen comes
in my room and we
hide under that overcoat on my bed.
Nobody can get us there.

Old Watson'll want me homework tomorrow and I haven't done it.
He's bloody had it!  I hate that bloody school.

# TOO TIRED TO ARGUE

I see the boy and girl droopy-eyed watching satellite TV.
Mustn't go to bed 'til she gets home.
She left money for some chips and curry sauce from Bert's chippie
and a packet of Jaffa cakes on the table.

Eyes prickling,
Cushion sticking a feather into his face.
Kicking his sister.

He wanted the rocker not the settee.
She too tired to respond,
Dozes.

Finger playing with the hole in the chair arm making it larger.
The bubbles in the lamp on the television twist and turn.
Too tired to argue now.
Margaret's asleep.
People look like they're dead when they're asleep.

The rattle of the door,
The opening.
She comes in and covers him with a coat.
Breath smelling sour,
Beer breath.
The man stands in the shadows waiting.
The stairs creak as they go up.
Voices above muffled.

Coat collar soft on his chin.

Silence.

Margaret stirs, asks where their mother is.
He points upwards.
Margaret nods.
Eyes close again.

He'll be gone next morning, they always are.
That's tomorrow
Sleep now ...

# THE RAINBOW

It's a strange world the world where children live.

I suppose to those who did not know the redbrick walls and regimented windows and endless cobbles and gas lamps and lavatory yards –
The streets all seemed the same.
They were not.

Here was a raging river or a jungle dense and impenetrable, a bloody battlefield, a western shanty town.
It depended what was showing at the Pictodrome that week.

But it was best when we went to the hills.
Racing up and down the grey shale undulations between the brickyard stables and the cast iron boiler by the quarry,
Fighting the Sioux or the Germans.

We kept out of the big brickfield where the great brickyard horses were tethered.
Brown and black and white they were, with shaggy feathers and untidy manes, smelling as horses smell.
They pulled the creaking two-wheeled carts up Windmill Hill.
Tealey the hossman drove them,
Wearing a harding apron and walking with a limp.
He cursed us for our cheek and spat when he smoked his pipe.
But we never did cheek him,
He frightened us too much.

We duffed to walk the Death Path along the walls of the disused delph.

We scrambled over and hid behind the great slabs of grey stones
dumped near the overgrown entrance to the tunnel, half hidden
by couch grass and willowherb.
We only once went down the tunnel;
There was a well in the middle and rats as I remember.
It was dark and damp
And we only went down there once.

Here on the hills we played a thousand violent games of war,
And killed and was killed and counted to ten and killed again until
bedtime.

One day stood out.
A Saturday it was as I remember.
We were free to roam the hills
And leap the puddles the rain had left behind flooding the dull,
clay paths.
Over the city a rainbow broke from Heaven.
We stopped and tried to see where it fell on the buildings of the
many-spired market in the town.
We said it must have been like that when Jesus was born,
I remember we thought he might be born again that night in
Leeds.
I don't think he was though,
At least we never heard he was.

It's funny that over all those years I remember that rainbow on
that Saturday afternoon.

It is a strange world, the world where children live.
Strange what they remember.

# MY MAM'S
# BOYFRIEND

My mam's boyfriend said we couldn't stop there anymore.
There was a lot of shouting.
There's was always a lot of shouting.
I don't like it when they shout.

My mam put everything in that old suitcase
And tied some string round it.
Our Les wanted to take his bike
But my mam said, *No.*
He could only take his playstation.

He had to carry that funny case with the handle that pulls out.
It's broken and he said he didn't want to.
She said he had to.
So he did and moaned all the way.

I had two Asda carriers.
One had all our Becky's clothes in
And that thing the doctor gave her.
She puts it over her mouth when she has a 'do'.
It's a funny thing.
She doesn't like it.
Mam says it does her good.

Gaz just stood watching us.
He said nowt.
He just looked.
My mam said, *You bastard.*

He said, *Piss off and take your fucking kids with you.*

So we went.

# KYLE

They called him Kyle;
So doing they could raise him from the debris of humanity in
which he lived.

He never knew his father.
His mother knew his father –
But she could never remember whether it was George or Kev or
Pizzie.

Pregnant she waddled to the DSS
Smoking her twenty a day
Feeding on crisps and chocolate
Finishing the night with a pint of lager and a double gin.

He tumbled from her womb
Easily
And grew stunted in size
With a wheezing chest and a cast blighting his right eye.

She gave him crisps and chocolate
And called him Kyle
– To give him a chance in life.

I saw Kyle last week outside the Oxfam shop
A tattoo'd line around his neck,
Arms a blaze of reds and blues and writhing naked bodies and
lions' heads.
I saw him outside the Oxfam shop pushing a pram;
With him a woman, pregnant – girl more like she was –
Dragging a pale faced toddler.

I wondered what they called the baby in the pram,
The pale faced toddler,
The innocent yet unborn.

Give them exotic names
That it will break the mould.

# AND WHERE
# WAS GOD?

They told us God was everywhere –
In the old classroom with the tiered steps and the coke stove by
the teacher's desk,
They said He was there.
I never saw Him.

They looked shocked when we didn't know what happened on
Good Friday.
But nobody ever told us.
And when they did tell us
I never liked this God they talked about.
Imagine, giving His son to be nailed to a cross –
My dad would never have given me to be nailed to a cross.
They said He did it to save us from our sins.
My dad would have found another way.

I know we pushed caterpillars through Mrs Cowling's letterbox
And gave Bobby Dalby laxative to eat – telling him it was
chocolate.
If that was a sin, we would have said we were sorry.
There was no need to nail anybody to a cross.

They said we had to pray with our eyes closed and not peep.
Gordon Kitchingman peeped.
Nothing ever happened to him.

They read us poems about gardens rich in flowered scents and
vivid colours

And spoke in rhyme of bees on summer afternoons and hollyhocks and honeysuckle.
We'd never seen hollyhocks and honeysuckle.

We were born of the town
Of the soot and the grime,
Of the chimneys and the echoing cobbled setts.

There *was* grass there.
It grew between the cobbles and the gas tar.
It grew behind the old tin church amid the willowherb and privet hedge run wild.
There were bramble bushes at the bottom of the field where the brickyard horses ran amok after a day's work hauling carts up Windmill Hill.
But this was not the world of God they talked about at school,
His wonders to behold.
Some of the older people in the streets talked about God, as I remember.
Not the God of the church but the God of the chapel –
The Methodists and the Wesleyans and the Primitives down the hill.
And sometimes they whispered talk of Mrs Hogan and her daughter – *Roman Catholics*!
And, we fearful of dreads unimaginable, ran past their door when we went down that street.

The women talked of God in hushed tones on funeral days when the black hearse came,

Wrapping their pinnies around their arms to show respect and taking in the washing that hung across the street and drew the curtains.
They whispered in reverential tones,
*He works in strange ways.*

I never saw God in the streets.
I saw the Salvation Army humping great silver euphoniums and

playing carols sweetly at Christmastime.
I saw the Wesleyans come Whitsuntide push their organ on a
handcart bringing their hymns out of the chapel.
They always played beside the fish and chip shop, I remember.
But God never came with them.

If God was meant to be everywhere – then He forgot the streets.
There was no God in the streets
Only cobbles and gas lamps and row upon row of soulless redbrick
houses,
The barracks of the people, housing an army of sad humanity.

Some did go to find this God.
In the chapel by the pillar box opposite the Commercial Inn,
They came and sang with the fervour of Methodists and held
socials on Saturdays at seven;
Drinking orange juice and dancing waltzes to an old gramophone.

I don't know whether God went there.
I never went to a social.

Now I wonder at the flowers and marvel at a seagull's wheeling
flight
And watching the September sun slip down the reddening sky
I see how God can be everywhere.

There were red sunsets over the streets long ago
But I don't remember seeing God there.

# WALKING IN
# THE RAIN

I like to walk in the rain,
To feel the freshness on my face.
There is an excitement to stand alone with the elements,
To sense the wind and rain,
Darkness about and silence.
And I remembered,
As the lights across the valley,
Like fallen amber stars, winked in the wind.
I remembered that time in Standard Four.

The classroom was raked rising in huge steps with a gong hanging
above the door that Mr Atkinson, our headmaster, rang to tell the
school it was playtime.
It was the room where they showed us those jerky black and white
films of horses ploughing and sou'westered fisherman on sloping
trawler decks,
And huge retorts spluttering molten steel and farm labourers
scattering seeds by hand.

I remember the day Mr Atkinson came in.
He spoke to the teacher and then turned to us.
What was it we most liked to do, he asked.

I said walking in the rain, feeling the gentle drizzle on my face.
He smiled.
The others looked at me and said I was daft –
No-one likes to walk in the rain!

I did.
I still do.

# TOWN HALL MAN

A grey faced clerk he was,
Spending a lifetime under the shadow of the old Town Hall.
Penning neat notes
Of coke deliveries to council schools.
On Fridays he arranged his piles of pink and blue dockets alphabetically,
And watched the seasons flit by from a third floor window where the starlings perched.

He cycled every day to work;
Every day for forty-seven years –
Except when winter blizzards made him walk in brown galoshes.

They say he played at cricket in his youth,
Bowling fast for a local team.
Another Bowes or so they said
But a broken ankle on an office trip to Blackpool
Ended all that.

He never married.
Lived with his mother till she died in the January cold of nineteen forty-seven.

He never went on holiday
Except for an occasional weekend or so in a caravan at Filey.
Preferred to cycle Sundays in the Dales
And spent his weekdays writing neat notes of coke deliveries.

A lifetime spent under the shadow of the old Town Hall.
A quiet man he was.

Lonely within and without.
But happy that he knew where a badger's sett was hid,
Where pepper saxifrage grew,
And smiled to himself
That others were in ignorance.

Four people were at his funeral
Including the pastor
Who didn't even know him.

# OLD WOMAN ON A STREET CORNER

Back hooked
Fingers arthritic clutching her stick,
Waiting on the kerbside for a green man to bleep
To cross to the post office for her Monday morning pension.

A world she does not understand flows by.
There's nothing nice anymore.
Everything busy and noisy and even children swear in the street and use words
Only men used in taprooms once upon a time.

Nowadays she waits.
For what?
For the pain in her hip to begin again?
For the letter from her son in New Zealand that never comes?

Fourteen years of widowhood gone by.
He was a good man in his way.
But she remembered the dark days when he was not.
Remembered memories of things she wanted to remember,
That never truly were,
But she believed they had been, might have been.

Seventy-eight years old and her feet bad, and her back bad and never seeing anybody
One day to the next.

She reads the deaths column in the *Evening Post* every night.

So many now have gone on.
So few left.

Likes a nice bit of fish done in milk for Friday tea.

Logical positivism and minimalism,
Solzhenitsyn and McLuhanism,
Plath and Pollock.
Mean nothing to her.
She likes her tele
But why do they have the music so loud and gabble when they talk.

God works His wonders strangely.
And she says a prayer each night eyes closed as she'd been taught at Sunday school.
It's too hard to get to the Methodist Church on Town Street now.
At Christmastime they come in a car and take her to the carol service.
They forgot last year.
Everyone's so busy nowadays.

From her council flat you can see the roses bursting in the park now.
There were roses in that park when she was a girl.

Tomorrow is Tuesday and then Wednesday, then Thursday
And then Friday and …..

# THE THUMBPRINT OF METAPHYSICS

The thumb print of metaphysics, at least it is to me,
This scuffed, dull backed book
My father carried in his pocket
Up Windmill Hill to the brickyard kilns
Where the toppling over chimneys stood.

There where the kilns opened their angry mouths
Howling in pain to show a glimpse of Hell,
Of raging reds and glowing whites,
And ghostly shapes dancing in the flames behind the great sealed
door,
He fed those fires,
Then rested.

Here on dark, dull nights,
Around the solitude of midnight time
When the crickets sang in anxious chorus,
He sat in a wooden cabin
Drinking thick tea from a cracked pint pot
And read philosophy.

Struggled to make sense of words
Revealing hidden truths of life denied to ordinary men.
Words of great intellect,
Written by men at neat oak desks, viewing from their chintzy
windows, rolling lawns and rich delphiniums in herbaceous
borders.

They wrote with women's hands, soft and velvety,
Born of turning pages.

He turned pages, too.
Hands calloused,
Cracked by winter frosts
Revealing dark red flesh he salved with Vasoline.

And under the canopy of the stars
Hearing the heat of Hell,
He turned the pages
Seeking eternal truths,
And left his thumb print
On a coaldust covered book.

# TELEPHONIST

Mrs Mountford shrieks each day,
Every day;
Four children taking no bloody notice
And her worrying about Shane wanting a new Leeds United strip
for his birthday to be like other kids
And Edwin not reading at seven –
He must be bloody daft – Maureen was reading at just turned five.
At school they say don't worry.
But she does worry.
They need to learn,
They don't want to end up like her,
A forty year-old nobody

She worries.
She worries every day,
It's the way she is.
Not outwardly, inwardly;
When the wind whips at night across the rooftops
And she tosses and turns in an empty bed
And wonders if he's found another woman,
*The bastard* –
She's welcome to him!
Yet still she aches inside for him
And hates herself for the aching.

Sometimes it's worse than others
The loneliness.
No-one to talk to about Marueen's adenoids;
No-one to talk to,

To feel support from,
No-one.
And the crying comes.
She hates herself for being so bloody soft.
Yet still she cries
But into the pillow so the children can't hear.

Brazen Millie Mountford they call her.
Millie with her too tight skirt
And blonde hair showing dark roots.

Millie, cigarette dangling,
Serves daily behind the bar of the Rising Sun
Giving as good as she gets,
Eleven 'til three when the children come home.

They'd never speak to proper ladies like that.
Doesn't bother her –
Why should it?
She's no lady,
And men are all bastards, anyway
They're only after one thing.

On Tuesdays and Thursdays she works six 'til twelve,
A telephonist,
Mother babysitting.

Earning that bit extra to pay for
Cigs and school trips and whatever.
Telephonist she calls it to other people.
Answering queries about lost cheque cards,
She says when asked.
Her mother guessed but said nothing.

A sex chat line it was.
*And if the buggers get fresh I slam the phone down on 'em.*
*Piss heads.*

Talking endlessly

To sex-starved men,
Filling their fantasies over a telephone line,
Hearing them masturbate their satisfaction
To her words.
Only words and sounds to excite them.
Nothing else.

It's a living
Bringing in that bit more.
Paying for the extras.
It's not like being there,
Being touched,
Seeing them.
It's only words.
It's all they've got
Poor sods.
Just words.

# MAN AND BOY

I sat beside an old man yesterday
And saw the boy within the man.
The years had seared his face telling through the craggy lines the story of a life;
Well spent or wasted?
The voice mellowed in drink laughed long, full of energy and élan.
The eyes, those windows of the soul, revealed the inner being
Broken within as withered without.

We sat and reminisced, speaking of long gone summers and schoolboy days and friends,
Names now forgotten but they themselves remembered.
He laughed and I remembered his laughter as a boy
And wondered how he went on laughing when his face and eyes spoke so
Of despair and destitution.

But I saw him as he was full sixty years ago
Laughing and I remembered his laughter.
I looked on him and saw the boy within and felt a sadness at the waste.
Or was it waste?

What did he think when he looked at me I wonder?

# KING THURSDAY

He had no parents, none he ever knew.
His mother died in childbirth, his father's name only a rumour.
A neighbour brought him up
Sending him with her own to the council school,
Dressing him, like them, in cast-offs she'd had given.

And he, Sunday-and-weekday-alike, never had new clothes until his first long trousers
The week he started work.

Butcher-boy at the Co-op
Pedalling a bike with orders round the streets.
They sacked him for being late and serving meat with unwashed hands
And never knew of the ten bob notes he secretly lifted from the till
Hiding them between the straps of his braces.

He became a man.
Twelve pints Friday night.
Same again Saturday.
Rolled dogends Tuesday till Friday-pay-day

When the urge grew great
Caught a bus to town,
Picked up a Robin Hood woman smelling of cheap perfume and gin
Paid for twenty minutes unsatisfactory relief.

Lost his job when the asbestos factory closed
And never worked again.

Survived on beans and tomato sausage, cigarettes and beer.
What else worthwhile was there?

The day he collapsed the doctor told him he would kill himself if
he went on like that.
Discharged himself from hospital
And went on.

Why not?
In a godless world only the fool fears death.
He chose his destiny – fulfilling his abandonment.
Was satisfied if satisfaction can be found.
Sartre's words of wisdom born of the Sorbonne and a hundred café
conversations
discovered existential truths.
He found them in one council school and a dozen taprooms over
fifty years
Without searching.

His body, stench invested, shuffled to draw his social every
Thursday
And for a day he lived like a king.
Drunk from eleven till eleven.
Nirvana for the godless in a soulless, hopeless life.
What else is there?

# THE GOLDEN RULE

He waited in the New Inn taproom
Standing silently at the bar
Smoking a Capstan;
His hand on a pint of Melbourne mild.
Waiting.

The landlord knew him, said nothing;
Bustled busily behind the bar, pulling off after putting a new barrel on.

Little Benjie the paperman stood at the window with a pint of mixed
Looking,
Waiting for the number sixteen tram and the afternoon *Evening Post*s
And the racing results.

The landlord hummed.
Benjie kept peering down as far as Whingate Junction.
The clock over the fireplace tock-ticked.
The man at the bar checked his half-hunter.
Said nothing.
Waited.

The tram wires began to dance.
And then with a clanging and a whining
The number sixteen arrived at the terminus.

The man said nothing.
Benjie humped the papers from the driver's platform,

Dumped them on the taproom floor.

The man picked one up,
Looked at the stop press.
Face impassive.

Bookies need impassive faces
When gambling's illegal and men pass crumpled pieces of paper
from grubby hand to grubby hand on street corners.
*Two bob each way and keep a look out.*

But you should lay off bets.
Always lay off bets that get too big.
That's the golden rule.
The golden rule of bookies –
Never gamble.
Lay them off.

He hadn't.
Nightjar had won.
He'd lost.
Lost everything.
Couldn't pay.

He downed the Melbourne mild
And went out silently,
Walking the long walk
To the canal.
Passed Gott's green park
And the power station,
Down to the canal.

They found his body two days later
Near the wharf by Armley Mills.

# THE FACE

She went about her business
Hurriedly;
Ignoring other shoppers,
Purposely.
Scurrying down Armley Town Street,
Darting from greengrocer's to the newsagent's,
Out of the dry cleaner's, into the butcher's.
People pretended not to see her
Not to notice.

Hair disregarded, unkempt.
Clothes ill-fitting.

Her face said it all.
A white plaster masking her nose contrasting the beaten, blue-
black, sallow, yellow eyes,
The puffed mouth said nothing.
The face said it;
Shrieked it.

In her silence
Her eyes spoke of beatings
Within as well as without.
Spoke of endless screamings when the money ran out and he came
home drunk on borrowed cash.
Spoke of the hurt when he kicked her.
Spoke of missing this week's club to buy Mandy some new
knickers,
Spoke of not walking down Stocks Hill for fear of meeting Mrs

Hardwick and having to tell her she couldn't pay her back once again.
Spoke of harrowing children
Nagging for this; wanting that.
Spoke of rising each morning knowing there was no escape.

Dull eyes that dreamed dreams that never could be.
Was this what it was all about?

And why me?

# THE DAY GANDHI DIED

I remember the day that Gandhi died.
A January Friday it was,
And we, the weekend ahead, waited for a Divinity lesson to begin.

She came in slowly, this dumpy, grey-haired lady,
The only woman teacher in a school of boys;
Employed to teach us the meaning of God.

She flopped on the chair by the huge teacher's desk on the raised
platform at the front.
Pulled her gown about her shoulders and spoke quietly;
*Boys, I cannot teach you today, Mr Gandhi has been assassinated. You
must occupy yourselves this afternoon.*

It met nothing to us.
We'd heard of Gandhi, seen this spindly-legged man wrapped up
in a white bundle on newsreels at the pictures.
I remember my mother talking to my father about Gandhi fasting.
It made no sense to me.
So we had no Divinity lesson that Friday afternoon.

Why a teacher should sit red-eyed, in silence
Locked in her thoughts,
Never occurred to us.

We didn't know we had lived through history in the making,
Or witnessing a kindly woman in mourning for someone she had
never met,

Spoke more of Divinity than any lesson we would ever have.

# IN SILENT SOLITUDE

I whispered in the craggy coves, above the sound of lapping waters and the call of gulls,
When the breakers explode on the seaweed stones and shower salt sea abroad
Like the double handed sower flecking his seeds across the bare brown earth.

My words are lost and the sound of shibboleths are silent.
I speak on the windswept fells of dun, dry heather where the curlew circles and the hawk awaits.
I cry out loud amidst the city bedlam of heaving engines and the endless torrents of meaningless mouthings that permeate the ether.

And sitting silently,
In solitude
I ponder these things
Alone.

# PAGLIACCI

I remember him as one of stunted growth,
Woodbine dripping from his bottom lip,
Eyes globulous and bloodshot;
A broad strap holding up his trousers –
Half-mast trousers they were that made us laugh.

Laboured six days a week heaving barrows at Ingham's brickyard;
Working nights in a local fish shop chopping chips and swilling
out the fish cellar with a rubber hosepipe.

Signed his name with a stilted signature,
Following each word with a move of his tongue,
Licking the end of his copying-ink pencil every six letters.

Never read a book, as I remember, save the odd cowboy novelette
from the library in the spice shop at the corner of Tadcaster Street
and Whingate Road.
Enjoyed his rugby at Barley Mow
Cheering on the Villagers,
Boasted to us of seeing Harold Wagstaff and the greats of gone-by
days.

And he listened to Pagliacci,
Standing in the gods at the Grand Theatre when the opera came.

Transported to another world
Found in the voice of a clown
His own soul too had wings.
Found in the haunting arias
An inner being transcending everything he knew,

Bathing his soul with an iridescent majesty of sound,
Freeing his spirit for a moment of tranquillity,
Ethereal peace.

We laughed at him for liking opera,
For listening to words in a language he could not understand.

We never realised, words have no meaning
To the soul.

He in his world of sweat and toil and daily bewilderment
Sensed what we with all our wit failed to recognise.

And he sucking his Woodbine
Simply called us
*Daft.*

# THE CARIBBEAN MAN

They found him three days before Christmas.
He had been dead a week.
They found him stiff and cold and alone.

Their flashlights flicked across the room picking out the unwashed dishes by the sink;
The tumble of bedclothes in the corner that did for a bed;
The empty rum bottles on the table.
And the ivory crucifix on the wall ignored it all.

There was a gasfire, dirty and unused, waiting repair;
They cut the electricity off five weeks ago.

For the most part he managed, eating from unheated tins,
Finding his peace in cheap rum.

His hair was grey and neatly curled as you would expect of a Caribbean man.
His ebony face was etched with lines of suffering,
Not age.

He was born to suffer
Within and without.

His jaw sagged open as if wanting to ask a question.
And was this all it had been about?
    – to graft while the hands were calloused, the fingers gnarled;
To sail a thousand miles from a shanty in the tropics

And die on a dismal December day in the garret of a northern English town?

What did he think of in those final moments,
What did he hope for?
Or did he just rejoice
It was all over?

# ONE O' THEM

You could never tell people, that was the trouble.
You had to keep it to yourself.

I didn't realise when I was at school.
I did what the others did;
Played football, not very well.
Couldn't see the point of it.
When I was a teenager went out with a couple of girls.
Couldn't see the point of that.

I was in my twenties when I realised.
Group of us from college had gone to the Lake District.
That's when I realised, I think.
Of course you couldn't tell anybody in those days.
It was illegal.
Now it's legal
And you still can't tell anybody.

I was thirty-one when I went to live with Alex.
That's when my family guessed.
My mother never mentioned it.
Pretended she didn't know.
She knew all right.
I once remember overhearing her saying it would have killed my
father had he lived to find out.

Our Janice understood.
Her husband didn't.
Said I was *one o' them*.
Didn't want me near his kids.

Somebody found out in the office.
I don't know how.
But it all changed then.
Not that anything was said.
Just looks and sniggers.
Sinclair said I should make a formal complaint.
It wasn't worth it.
I just left.

We had a good life Alex and me.
Thirty-seven good years.
Did a lot together.
Then he got a brain tumour and died.

Our Janice understood, she said how sorry she was.
My mother just said, *Oh*.

# WHY?

There were two of them,
Punching and kicking the huddled form on the ground.
When I stopped the car,
They gave one last kick
And ran off.

It was a student from the university lying there,
Battered and bruised.
His new white raincoat
Bloodied and mud stained.

I took him back to school and we patched him up
And tried to clean his coat as best we could.

*Why?* I asked.

He looked at me,
Puzzled that I should ask.

*I'm black*, he said.

# ON GOLDEN DAYS

On golden days,
On gentle autumn days,
When morning mists herald in a glowing sun,
I forget the torment of the mind, the ceaseless fury of the soul
And see in the russet trees of distant Farnley
The promise of age.

The year is growing old.
The callow times of frivolous, pastelled spring and vibrant summer hues are gone.

It's the time of subtler shades and yesterday's people.
A time to view the vision of tomorrow,
And the time of lives long lived, reborn for the coming dawn.

The sheep, in the fields behind the farm across the valley, forage in ignorance.
An unseen dog barks its lonely bark.

As the apotheosis of our being unfolds before us
We realise immortality, leaping from our loins,is fruitfully fulfilled.

And lasting love itself,
Embracing horizons unimagined in the youth time,
Offers the silent purity of the stars.

# MRS CRANNAGE

She waddled across the street,
Crossing by the lamp post and the lavatory yard.
Her black dress sweeping the cobbles as she moved,
And made her way, flat-capped,
To the New Inn by the tram terminus.

There in the passageway she tippled thick, black stout,
Just one.
Regular as clockwork,
Then back she came
To sit in the dark by the fire and watch pictures in the flickering
flames.

The children, noisy and unkempt,
Knocked at her door and ran away;
Pushed caterpillars through her letterbox;
Stole her milk.
She screamed at them not to do it again.
They took no notice,
And did it again

On good days they ran errands for her
And waited on the doorstep for the promised penny-for-going.
They never went in.
It stank inside with the smell of old women.

One day I had to go in.
I can't remember why, but I had to go in.
I remember it was dark and I tried to hold my breath.

On the side board a huge glass dome stood.
Inside were two stuffed birds,
I can't remember what they were,
Only they were two stuffed birds,
And the dome was filled with poppies.
Red poppies.
Remembrance poppies.
She put a new one in every 11 November,
For Fred.

On the wall by the cellar head where she
Kept her milk cool on summer days,
A picture hung.
That was Fred,
Her son,
A young soldier, peak-capped and bandoliered.

They said he'd been killed at Passchendale.
She knew he hadn't.
She once saw a newsreel at the Pictodrome and Fred was there
marching in it.
She knew he'd come home one day,
But she'd put a poppy in the dome every November until he did.

# FAILURE

What does a woman say when she sees failure written on his face?
She has lived with him,
Been married to him, fifty years or more
But she cannot bring herself to say it; to admit it.
She knows he cannot face it.

When she met him long ago at the Empress Ballroom
One hot Saturday night of a long forgotten July,
They quick stepped and tangoed
To the Empress Seven.
She still remembered his Brycreemed hair and slim body
And fresh freckled faced and fetching smile.

He wasn't the cleverest in their group,
Or the most handsome,
Or one with the flash MG sports car,
Or captained the local cricket club and got his name in the paper,
Or had the best collection of Bill Haley forty-fives.
And he hesitated when decisions had to be made.

But she loved him for his gentleness and his understanding.

He promised her *he would get on*.
She watched through the years
And knew he'd never get on.

She never quite understood what he really did.
She listened to him complaining about Rixby in Accounts
And the Despatch Department and the poor designs that would never sell.

And the new young fools from university that came with no experience.
He sneered at their jargon jaberwocky about H. Rs. and down-sizing and re-defining.
The women some of them – bright eyed and efficient –
Frightened him in their intolerance of inefficiency.

And why change things that had worked for thirty years?
Changes not for the better.
He tried to adapt.
For three months he agonised when they introduced computers.
But he tried to adapt.

They complimented him on the Grogan account;
Praised his efforts on the way he handled the Bayeux fiasco.
But when it came to promotion
There was always someone brighter, someone with the skills they just happened to be looking for at that moment;
Someone more articulate with his ear to the ground and aware of the New Vision.

She watched now how he sat before the TV
Not seeing,
His eyes lost in the mists of yesteryear, long lost dreams of what might have been.

Occasionally he would say there might be a chance if Robertson were moved to the Bradford branch or Illingworth got kicked upstairs
Or Summersby took early retirement.

But she knew there would be no chance really.
Perhaps once there had been when the Customer Response Department had been established
But they gave it to Delphine MacIntyre.
She often wondered if he hadn't had that heavy cold the day of the interview,
If he hadn't worn that brown tie and the shirt with the buttons on

the collar.
Would he have been appointed?

Deep down she knew the truth just as she knew the chances had
all gone by.
And deep in his soul, he knew, and knew she knew.
But he sat silently and said nothing.

# TORMENT

I only saw her once.
A neat woman she was,
Hair white, softly shaped,
Walking stoop shouldered now that arthritis gouged her joints.
But her eyes sparkled belying pain and age,
Sparkled with the joy of long gone days.

She spoke with the clipped precision of an educated woman.
Professional perhaps.
I never did find out which profession.
She had the bearing of one who had shouldered responsibility
Easily,
Enjoying Vivaldi and Trollope to relax herself.

She lost everything when her husband died.
The large house with the great willow tree,
The antique furniture that had been her mother's,
Everything.
She didn't know of the debts.
He'd never told her.

And now this woman of poise was come here
To an old people's home run by the council.
And being a newcomer
Must share a room.

***

I only saw her once.
A dull-faced woman she was.

Cardigan soup-stained and half-fastened.
Hair steel-grey and uncombed.
Eyes languid; voice bitter and harsh,
Hardened by a thousand altercations.
Language coarse,
Toughened by the vicissitudes of life.
Born in poverty, to die in poverty.
Untutored.

But her room in the council home was warm and the food was fair.
There was TV in the lounge and Bingo on a Friday night.
But being new she had to share a room.
She didn't like sharing with the snob

*Stuck up bitch.*
Anyway there was always Bingo on Friday.
The snob can go to hell!

The snob enjoyed Friday evenings
Alone,
Listening to Question Time and Alistair Cooke
As she had done through the years.
She dreaded the footfalls but always managed to smile when the
door opened and
Bingo had finished.

*The snob can go to hel*l.
The snob had gone to hell.
And I wondered why it had to be.

# THE FLYING
# FORTRESS

He sat befuddled in a geriatric home
Fly undone,
Eyes staring into a vacant limbo land,
Mouth dripping dried boiled egg from forgotten breakfast time.
Vaguely aware of other shapes broken in body and mind,
Twisted wrecks of jettisoned humanity all around him.
Alone.
All day he sat quietly stroking his hands gently together.
And nobody knew.

He couldn't remember now.
Just vague memories of Central Park and Jim Sullivan.
Played against the cherry and whites he had.
The fastest forward in the Northern Union they said.
The Flying Fortress they called him.
Played at Headingley and Odsal.
Never played at Wembley.
Broke his arm in the semi-final against Huddersfield.
Missed the final.

Played for Great Britain.
Got seventeen caps.
Wonder what happened to them?

Then that injury at Parkside against Hunslet.
He never played any more.

Played fourteen years all told.

Club said it wasn't their fault.
They gave him ten pounds and wished him luck

Tried to run a pub but the so-called friends took him in,
Everybody wanting free drinks.
Then he worked in that warehouse in Dock Street.
But after that.
Nothing.

Can't remember, you see.
Memory manacled,
Living in a land of flitting shades and shadows.

And I wondered that quiet Sunday morning.
Watching him there.
Once cheered by thousands,
Now nothing,
A living testament to what?

# THE MEANING
# OF LIFE

On a windswept hillside they laid him to rest.
The town in the valley,
Shrouded in mizzle,
Ignored him –
And went about its business.
It never knew him.
The only time his name went in print was in the deaths' column of
the *Evening Post*.

The vicar mumbled the words
And forgot the name of the man he had never met
Except in death.

The mourners stood respectfully by.
Duty bade they hang their heads in solemn silence,
Wishing it were over,
Waiting for opening time.

The final rigmarole was done.
The final act of the farce called life played out – the tossing of a
clod of earth on the wooden coffin.

He considered church a hypocrisy all his life.
And yet –
*They bloody well get you in the end*, he always said.
They did get him in the end,
Wrapped up in a silken shroud
And chanting their meaningless mumbo-jumbo over him.

A miner he was
Of stunted growth,
His leg crippled in a roof-fall half a century ago.
Ended him playing wing-half for the Welfare at twenty-eight
years of age.

Foul-mouthed he was
Spluttering obscenities with every sentence – but never in front of
ladies –
And never in the best room only the taproom.

When they took him in intensive care that last time
A preacher came,
Dog-collared and soft speaking,
As preachers are.

Did he wish to talk of God and the meaning of life and salvation?

He told the dog-collar
*Bollocks!*
That was the meaning of life.

# GOLDEN WORDS
# OF BRASS

They speak golden words these prophets of tomorrow,
Bearing beatitudes of hope for a people weary of the wilderness of their time.
Their mealy mouthings echo falsely like the timbrels of dancing harlots and the brassy tongues of politicians.

Promises of tomorrow knowing there is ever only now.
Promises of tranquillity when the earthfires rumble and vomiting volcanoes hurl damnation on the peasant and his plough.
Promises of peace when banners beckon the young to bloody mutilation and a people's pride, blinded by ignorance and bigotry.
Destroys posterity.

Where is there hope? In Lidice or Srebrenica; in Sharpeville or the Shankhill Road?
Where are the skulls of Polpot, the ghosts of Lidice?

But who is there to care?

Should we find hope in the coming of the seasons; the promise of spring, washed with sweet rain heralding a fruitful summer?
Should we find it in the crying of a newborn, wrinkle red-faced and helpless, lying in its mother's arms?
Or do we find that germinal flicker of hope in the bosom of despair itself?
Find it in the bloody chaos wrought of a thousand conflicts, fashioned by the brutality of bigots?

From the apocalypse of history, hope will rise.
Mankind goes on and dreams.

It is good to dream when the fires of the winter cast long shadows.
We need not dream in the summer when the days are warm and
eternity is seen in the leafing of a tree.
Then we know and need no promises

# THE GODLESS TIME

They were born in the wilderness of the city
When God still lived;
Before the world changed,
Before the concrete jungle rose around bringing its stark barbarity
Into an ordered world.

Theirs was a wilderness:
A redbrick wilderness of house on house,
Endless streets,
Faceless and grit-grimed.
The redbrick chapels, the grey stone church,
Sentinels of the soul,
Stood in silent conflict,
Vying each other suspiciously.
The council school, and library, the Royal Oak and the New Inn,
And the Lyric Cinema where the programme changed every
Monday and Thursday,
All shrouded by the soot of a myriad chimneys.

Between the tram terminus and the public baths
A wasteland of dogmuck and debris.
And cobbled streets,
Where hung the echoes of a thousand pairs of clogs,
Ringing on dark winter mornings before the hooter of the mill or
factory broke the icy dark.

There were good days;
A chara to Blackpool for a treat, and the band playing every
Sunday in the park near the old speaker's stone.

This was the womb from which they crawled.
Lacking in beauty,
It held a strength
They never knew it had
Until it was lost.

They now look down
On a godless wilderness
A kindless place, where love has died and Mammon reigns supreme.
And worn out men, crooked backed and drawn-faced , cough the phlem of life and spit their souls away;
And sad-faced women shake their heads
And long for times that never truly were.

The godless time;
Born to live; and live they did – after a fashion.
Born to die; and die they will as it's foretold.
A welcome release from the endless, pointless toil.
The cassock draped priest smelling of incense spoke of purgatory and warned of worse to come.

There was no worse to come,
They had lived it.
The rest was sweet release.

# DAVID THORNTON

David Thornton was born in Leeds in 1935 and spent his entire professional life as a teacher and later head teacher there. He was born in one of the city's working-class back-to-back areas and still lives with his wife within a mile of his birth place. David is a historian, specialising in the history of Leeds and has published several academic books about the city as well as a wide range of children's picture story histories. For over twenty years David edited a cassette magazine for visually impaired people, and following his retirement was one of the editors of the Thoresby Society, the Leeds historical society. This is David's first published collection of poetry.

Printed in Great Britain
by Amazon

28287561R00046